YOUNG SCIENTISTS INVESTIGATE

Plants
Around Us

Malcolm Dixon
and Karen Smith

Evans

Evans Brothers Limited

NOTES FOR TEACHERS AND PARENTS

Plants around you (pages 6-7)
Through discussion and observation try to make children more aware of the variety of plants in their environment, especially in and around their home and school.

The stem (pages 8-9)
Adult help will be needed to cut a hole in the end of the cardboard box. Let children observe, daily, how the stem of the plant grows towards the light. Discuss their ideas of how the stem could be made to grow upwards. Let them set up the experiments to see which ones work.

The roots (pages 10-11)
It is important to note the safety warning and to ensure that hands are carefully washed after handling plants and soil. Encouraging the children to re-pot the plants will help to ensure respect for living things.

Leaves (pages 12-13)
Plants get their water and nutrients from the soil through their roots (see pages 10 and 11). Most plants do not grow well in shady places because they cannot get enough light for their needs.

Flowers (pages 14-15)
Illustrated reference books may be needed to find out the names of different flowers.

Flowers growing (pages 16-17)
Help children to find the outer ring of sepals and, inside them, the petals.

Seeds (page 18-19)
It may take a few weeks before the leaves appear.

Bulbs (pages 20-21)
If a bulb, such as a hyacinth, is unavailable then an onion can be used. Encourage children to observe closely as the shoots and roots grow.

Fruits and vegetables (pages 22-23)
Adult help will be needed to draw a graph of their results.

Trees (pages 24-25)
Help children to observe a range of tree trunks. Can they put their arms around them? Deciduous trees lose their leaves in winter. Evergreen trees retain their leaves throughout the year.

Water (pages 26-27)
The flower sucks up the coloured water from the vase and the petals of the flower appear coloured. The water level decreases as the flower sucks up the water.

Plants and people (pages 28-29)
This spread is intended to promote an awareness, in young children, of the importance of plants to them in their everyday lives.

Contents

Plants around you

▲This plant grows in the hot desert.

◀ This plant grows in the cold Arctic.

There are millions of plants in the world. They grow almost everywhere, even in very hot and very cold places. Plants use sunlight to make their own food. Without plants we could not live.

Some plants have flowers. Other plants such as seaweeds, mosses and ferns never have flowers.

Do you have plants in your home? Do you have plants in your school? Many people find it relaxing to have plants around them.

Work with a friend

Take a small plastic hoop and lay it on a patch of ground. How many different kinds of plants can you find inside the hoop? Draw some of the plants that you find. In what ways are these plants similar? In what ways are they different?

 You will need: small plastic hoop drawing paper pencils clip-boards

The stem

The stem of a plant usually grows upwards with the leaves towards the light. If a plant is in the shade then the stem will grow long so that the leaves reach the light. Inside the stem of a plant there are narrow tubes. These carry water and food around the plant.

Look at the stems of some plants. Are they soft or hard? Are they short or long? Are they rough or smooth? Are they straight or twisty?

Reaching for light

Cover the inside of the box and lid with black paper.
Cut a small hole in one end of the box.
Water the plant and place it inside the box as shown in the small photograph.
Fit the lid on the box. It must be a tight fit.
Place the box in a warm and light place.
Take off the lid once a day and look inside.
Watch how the stem grows towards the light.

You will need:
a cardboard box
black paper
sticky tape
plant (runner bean, for example) in a flowerpot
scissors

Find out more!
How could you make the stem grow upwards? Try out your idea to see if it works.

The roots

The roots of a plant hold it firmly in the soil so that it is not easily pulled out or blown over by the wind. The roots take in water, which the plant needs to make its food and to grow.

The children in the photograph are looking at some of the roots of a tree. These roots are very strong. They can push through the soil searching for water, and they anchor the tree. Look out for tree roots like these.

Observe the roots of a plant

Place some old paper on a table. Carefully pull one of the plants from its pot. Remove soil from around the roots. Now look closely at the roots of the plant. What colour are they? How many are there? Are they all the same thickness?

What else have you noticed? Are the roots of the other plant similar to the first? Remember to carefully replace the plants in their pots after you have finished with them.

You will need:
two small pot plants
old paper

⚠ **Wash your hands after handling plants and soil.**

Leaves

Leaves grow out from the stem of a plant. They use light, water and a gas, called carbon dioxide, from the air around them to make food for the plant. The food is carried around the plant — to the flowers, stem and roots — in a watery syrup called sap. Why is it that most plants do not grow so well in shady places? Where do plants get their water from ?

Work with a friend

Collect about ten leaves from different plants. Talk about the ways in which the leaves are similar and the ways in which they are different. Try to answer these questions:

Which leaf is the smallest?
Which leaf is the biggest?
Do any of the leaves have the same shape?
Which leaf is the thinnest?
Which leaf is the thickest?
What colours are the leaves?
Are any of the leaves shiny?
Do any of the leaves have sharp edges?

What can you say about all of the leaves?

Flowers

Flowers have many different shapes, colours and scents. Look out for circular-shaped flowers. Can you find some bell-shaped flowers? What other shapes can you find? How many colours can you see? Smell the scent of some flowers. Do all flowers smell?

Make a pressed-flower collection

Place a piece of blotting paper on a piece of card. Put some flowers on to the blotting paper and place more blotting paper and card on top of the flower. Put some heavy books on top. Let the books press the flowers for about two weeks. Use clear glue to fix the pressed flowers to card. Make a collection of your favourite flowers.

You will need:
Some flowers
blotting paper
card
books
clear glue
scissors

Find out more!
Find out the names of the flowers in your collection and write them on the cards.

Flowers growing

Most flowers start as buds. Look at the bud in the photograph. Can you see the ring of green sepals on the outside? The sepals protect the flower as it grows. Inside the sepals you can see the red petals of the flower. The smell and colour of the petals attract bees and butterflies to the flower.

Make scent from flower petals

Place some petals from a flower in a small amount of cold water.
Use a spoon to stir the petals.
Can you smell the liquid?

Try to make scented water using petals from other flowers.

You will need:
flower petals (from scented flowers such as rose, violet or lilac)
water
plastic cups
spoons

Find out more!
Try crushing the petals in water.
Does this make a stronger scent?

Seeds

Many plants grow from seeds. Seeds need to be scattered away from their parent plants so that they have light and water to grow. Some seeds are moved by animals. Other plants, such as the dandelion in the picture, have their seeds spread to new growing areas by the wind. Plants such as the pea have pods which burst open and spread their seeds. A few plants even use water to spread their seeds.

Watch seeds grow

Leave some seeds in the small bowl of water for one night. Roll up some blotting paper and place it inside the plastic bottle. Wedge a few seeds between the plastic and the blotting paper. Add water to the bottle. Do not cover the seeds with water. Place the bottle in a dark place for a few days and then move it to a warm and light spot. Add water from time to time to keep the paper moist. The seeds take in water and start to grow.

You will need:
a cut-down plastic bottle
runner or broad bean seeds
blotting paper
jug of water
small bowl of water

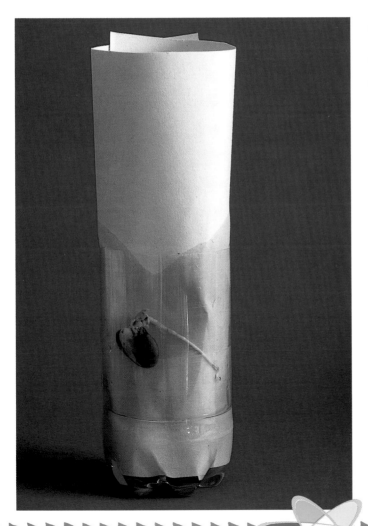

Watch as the roots grow downwards and the stem grows upwards. How many days is it before leaves appear?

Bulbs

Some plants grow from bulbs. Look at the photograph. All of these beautiful daffodils grew from bulbs. A bulb is a large bud which grows to form roots, leaves and flowers. Ask an adult to cut a bulb in half. You will see that it is made up of layers. This is where food is stored so that it can grow. An onion is a bulb. What will happen if you plant it in soil?

Watch a bulb grow

Ask an adult to cut the top part from a clear plastic bottle. Cut a hole in the centre of a piece of card. The hole should be large enough for the base of a bulb to sit in. Fill the bottle with water. Rest the card on the bottle and sit the bulb on the card. The base of the bulb must touch the water.

Now place the bottle and bulb in a dark place for about five weeks.

Then place them in a light position and watch how the bulb grows.

Make drawings to show how the bulb grows.

You will need:
a hyacinth bulb
clear plastic bottle
card
scissors
water

Fruits and vegetables

What is your favourite fruit? Which vegetables do you like? Fruits and vegetables help to keep us healthy. All fruits and vegetables come from plants. How many fruits and vegetables can you name in the photograph? Fruits contain seeds. Some fruits have one seed whilst other fruits have many.

Find the seeds

Remove the seeds from a collection of fruits and vegetables. You may need the help of an adult to cut some of the fruits. Count the number of seeds in each fruit. Record your results on a chart.
Use your results to draw a graph.

You will need:
some fruits and vegetables
knife
plastic spoons
paper plates

Find out more!
Do the biggest fruits have the most seeds?

Trees

A tree is a very tall plant. The stem of a tree is very strong. It has a special name — the trunk. The strength of the trunk allows a tree to grow taller than other plants. In this way the tree gets plenty of light. Look at the height of the trees in the photograph.

Look out for very tall trees near your home.

Looking at trees

This photograph was taken in late summer. What will the trees look like in the autumn, in the winter and in the spring?

Find a tree near your home. Observe this tree for a whole year. Use a notebook to draw some of the changes you notice.

Find out more! Some trees keep their leaves all through the year. What name do we give to these trees?

Water

All plants need water. They take water in through their roots and their leaves. Some plants need a lot of water. They grow in damp or boggy places. Some plants grow in water, in ponds and rivers. Seaweeds grow in the sea. Some are under water all the time.

Do you ever give water to the plants growing in your home or at school? Do some plants need more water than others?

Watch a flower suck up water

Fill the container, nearly to the top, with water. Add some drops of food colouring to the water. Put the flower in the vase. Pour some cooking oil on to the water. This stops water from the vase escaping into the air. Place a piece of sticky tape to show the level of the water. Look at the flower, every few hours, over the next day. What happens to the flower? Look at the water level.
Why has this happened?

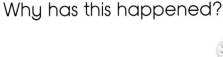

You will need:
cooking oil
narrow plastic container
food colouring
white flower
coloured sticky tape
water

Plants and people

All plants use sunlight to make their food. They use this food to grow stems, roots, leaves, flowers, fruits and seeds. In turn, we use plants for much of our food. Plants make the oxygen which we need to live. We use wood from trees to make buildings, furniture and paper. Plants are used to make cotton and linen clothing. Plants make our world a beautiful place to be. Can you imagine what the world would be like without plants?

Things that come from plants

Collect some magazines and catalogues with pictures in them.
Cut out pictures of things that come from plants.
Paste them on to large sheets of card.
Can you find pictures of furniture made of wood? Can you find pictures of beautiful places? How many plants can you see?

You will need:
magazines and catalogues
scissors
paste
large sheets of card

Find out more!
Make a list of all the things you use and eat, in one day, that come from plants.

Index